Praise for Ron Pad

"Wonderful, generous, funny poetry." —**John Ashbery**

"Reading Padgett one realizes that playfulness and lightness of touch are not at odds with seriousness. . . . As is often the case, leave it to the comic writer to best convey our tragic predicament."
—**Charles Simic,** *The New York Review of Books*

"For decades now, Ron Padgett has built up a body of work that, like the tenderly deadpan ballads of Jonathan Richman, has at its heart a sort of wry, pickled innocence. . . . The charm of his lines—and their power, because his work has a way of disarming you and pulling you in again and again—often comes from his allergy to anything pretentious or even 'poetic.' He makes plain niceness look like the most radical stance of all."
—**Jeff Gordiner,** *The New York Times*

"Padgett's plainspoken, wry poems deliver their wisdom through a kind of connoisseurship of absurdity." —*The New Yorker*

"Deeply pleasing to read." —*The Paris Review*

"I can think of no other poet I've read over the past 40 years who embodies Williams's spirit and his great heart's aesthetic. . . . I'm willing to put money on Padgett, in two or three generations (it takes that long) to be counted among the best poets of his generation, to be counted among the best American poets, period."
—**Thomas Lux, Poetry Society of America's William Carlos Williams Award**

"Forty-five years after *Great Balls of Fire,* Padgett's poems still fuel our capacity for joyful incomprehensibility and subsequent mobility of thought."
—*Poetry*

"Padgett's poems are so playful, self-mocking and eager to please that it would be easy to overlook their craft, not to mention the depth and sincerity of the emotions they convey. What animates [his work] is the tension between the buoyancy of its language and the gravity of its subject."
—*The Washington Post*

"Every page is a good time. . . . Sweet, hilarious, moving and mind-bogglingly imaginative. This book is for anyone who likes writing or who thinks it's interesting to have a mind (or simply a forehead)."
—**Richard Hell,** *The Wall Street Journal*

"These poems mingle the nervy sophistication and cosmopolitan experimentalism of a thriving international avant-garde art tradition with a kind of hillbilly twang that's unmistakably American."
—**Tom Clark**, *San Francisco Chronicle*

"A twentieth-century Great who is still producing superlative verse today. . . . And that's exactly what Padgett is: a virtuoso."
—**Seth Abramson**, *Huffington Post*

"Padgett's sense of romantic joy is undiminished, as is his thoughtfulness about language and the ways in which time changes meaning, and sense can morph into eloquent absurdity."
—**Ken Tucker**, *Entertainment Weekly*

"The poet makes superlative use of the directive writing consciousness—often automatic pilot—to tap the unconscious for memory, vision, emotion, and the unexpected and indefinable. The poems speak backwards and forwards in time, to self, to family and friends, to poetic technique, to the birds caged in the chest. It is so lovely."   —**Alice Notley**

"Ron Padgett makes the most quiet and sensible of feelings a provocatively persistent wonder."   —**Robert Creeley**

"The Ron Padgett of yore is still with us—as charming, unpretentious, and surprising as ever—but there is a new Ron Padgett in this book as well: a poet of heartbreaking tenderness and ever-deepening wisdom."
—**Paul Auster**

"Ron Padgett's poems sing with absolutely true pitch . . . agile and lucid and glad to be alive."   —**James Tate**

"Always discovering new pleasures and reviving old ones, full of what, in Frank O'Hara's phrase, 'still makes a poem a surprise,' Ron Padgett's poems, among those of our times, are in the small company of authentic works of art."   —**Kenneth Koch**

"Ron Padgett has that 'Lubitsch touch'—a whimsical grace that is full of wisdom and self-possession complete with mother-wit and, in his case, American invention."   —**Peter Gizzi**

DOT

Also by Ron Padgett
from Coffee House Press

Alone and Not Alone
Big Cabin
Collected Poems
Great Balls of Fire
How Long
How to Be Perfect
Joe: A Memoir of Joe Brainard
You Never Know

DOT

RON PADGETT

COFFEE HOUSE PRESS
Minneapolis
2022

Coffee House Press books are available to the trade through our primary distributor, Consortium Book Sales & Distribution, cbsd.com or (800) 283-3572. For personal orders, catalogs, or other information, write to info@coffeehousepress.org.

Coffee House Press is a nonprofit literary publishing house. Support from private foundations, corporate giving programs, government programs, and generous individuals helps make the publication of our books possible. We gratefully acknowledge their support in detail in the back of this book.

LIBRARY OF CONGRESS CATALOGING-IN-PUBLICATION DATA

Names: Padgett, Ron, 1942– author.
Title: Dot / Ron Padgett.
Description: Minneapolis : Coffee House Press, [2022]
Identifiers: LCCN 2022028550 (print) | LCCN 2022028551 (ebook) |
    ISBN 9781566896559 (paperback) | ISBN 9781566896566 (epub)
Subjects: LCGFT: Poetry.
Classification: LCC PS3566.A32 D63 2022 (print) | LCC PS3566.A32
    (ebook) | DDC 811/.54—dc23
LC record available at https://lccn.loc.gov/2022028550
LC ebook record available at https://lccn.loc.gov/2022028551

PRINTED IN THE UNITED STATES OF AMERICA

29 28 27 26 25 24 23 22   1 2 3 4 5 6 7 8

For Glen Baxter and Trevor Winkfield

Contents

A Note on the Title

How short can a title be and still be effective? Consider a title consisting of only one letter, as in the film *Z*. Could a title be even shorter than that? Aram Saroyan once published a "book" (in the form of a ream of blank typing paper) that had no title at all, but I'm not sure that having no title qualifies as a title. In any case, for such a small, unadorned word, *dot* has a lot of resonance for me.

When I was a child, Little Dot was one of my favorite comic-book characters. Every issue was devoted to her obsession with dots. It's impressive how much mileage the strip got from that one simple idea.

The first time I heard the term *polka dots* I imagined them dancing around, which, when you think of it, they sort of do.

The French word *dot* (dowry) struck me as disappointingly bare, as one would hope that a bride would bring to a marriage something more opulent.

When Joe Brainard read aloud from his work, he always said "dot dot dot" for ". . ." His doing so reflected the brilliant naivete of the work itself.

Then there's the crisp, pinpoint sound of the dot in Morse code, indicating *o,* which is visually rather dotlike itself.

When the internet arrived, I was struck by the use of the word *dot* in *dot com,* finally speculating that perhaps *period* and *decimal point* were too slow for the information superhighway. On the typewriter or computer keyboard, though, the dot, period, and decimal point look remarkably similar.

The actress June Brown, in the long-running British television soap opera *EastEnders,* portrayed my all-time favorite character, Dorothy Cotton, better known as Dot.

Many years ago, talking with my grandmother, I described a recurring dream I'd had for several decades, in which the only thing in my visual field was a dot that was infinitely far away, a dot that suddenly accelerated toward my head at incredible speed and abruptly stopped only inches from my face, where it was so enormous I could see nothing else, and then quickly began alternating between infinity and my face. My astonished grandmother said, "Why, Ronnie, I used to have that exact same dream! And I've never told a soul!"

Ultimately, though, my affection for this word might come from the moment in 1964 when Kenneth Koch, reading to me a line from one of my new poems—"at one of the numerous lunch counters which dot our city"—laughed and said, "Dot. That's a good word!"

DOT

Tea for You, Too

My friends,
I want to tell you
that in general things
are all right with me,
relatively speaking.
Just a second, here's Einstein
asking where the tea is.
I reassure him
it will be ready soon,
relatively speaking,
and he shuffles back
to the room that holds him,
with plenty of space
for that cup of tea,
even though the cup
is twelve feet in diameter,
about the same size
as my thinking of you
this morning.

Presto

Remember the guy
who sold magic tricks
in a small shop
next door to not
much of anything?
Of course you don't.
He made you disappear.

Starry Night

When I was in high school
I went out on a date
with a girl who looked
at the starry night sky
and blurted out
"Isn't nature *wonderful?*"
as if she had realized this
for the first time in her life.
I laughed in her face.
I wasn't wonderful.

Sonnet (Thunk)

In the back of my head I hear Kenneth Koch
saying, "Your poems are becoming simpleminded"
so I am going to let this one be more complex
and deeper than the blue ocean ever thought
of being. You think the ocean can't think?
It is forever making a large decision,
and it's always the same one,
like a bird opening its breast to the air
whose own breast is heaven,
like when something slams shut
with a muffled *thunk* in the dark
and we vibrate and wonder what vibration is
while hurling ourselves out of the fireworks
in the back of our heads where Kenneth isn't.

I Disobey

I look into the distance and see
Mei-mei Berssenbrugge
standing in the desert.
The wheels on her shoes
slowly wheel her away.
Some cardboard stars descend.
They too have shoes (cardboard ones).
"Don't go back!" the stars cry out,
but since my face is mashed
into wet concrete that tastes rather good,
I disobey.

The Long and the Short of It

I was all dressed up with no place to go
so I wandered around the streets for a couple of hours
looking at periods at the ends of sentences.
A long face on a long day.
The rain came down across the French poetry of the nineteenth
    century.
I was in Paris
in a cafe
operating the telephone.
A voice tells me my wife is pregnant.
I tell my wife.
We have a *grand crème*
and a big laugh.
Our child will be Made in France.

He had nothing to do with my long face,
in fact he considerably shortened it
by adding a comma here and there
and striking out across wide fields of parenthetical expressions
as the stars fled before him.

But my face was stuck on the front of my head,
so consciousness stepped forward and blew a bugle,
and soon ideas were jitterbugging
in and out of each other, creating
abstraction, just as the various woes
of the world blend to make me feel abstract,
like a Gorky, maybe, or the feeling you get
when you aren't suffering enough
and *il n'y a plus de Popeye aujourd'hui*
and my friends accelerate up the chimney like sparks.

Taboo

The first time I encountered the word *taboo* was in a
book—I think it was in Margaret Mead's *Coming of Age in
Samoa*—around the age of fourteen, and though the word's
context gave me a vague idea of what it might mean, I wasn't
sure, because the idea of something forbidden was in danger of
being drowned out by the sound of native drums in the night.
That is, the exoticism of the double-*o* ending had a strong
effect on me, conjuring up thatched huts, dense trees, bonfires,
and a gibbering witch doctor whose painted face and bizarre
headdress flickered in the firelight. *Taboo* was from a deep,
dark, primitive zone of the human psyche, a demonic version
of *forbidden* and *unlawful*. But it smelled good. That is, if it
were the same thing as Tabu, a perfume my mother used. Or
were taboo and Tabu two entirely different things, like a boat
in water and a boat in poker?

   Then I learned that Sigmund Freud—I thought his name
was pronounced *Frood*—had written a book called *Totem and
Taboo*. A few years before that I had seen his name in a comic
book that alluded to him in a way that suggested there was
something naughty about him, you know, *s-e-x*. (Yes, in those
days some people didn't dare say the word, they spelled it out.)
Associated with Freud, *taboo* started to take on a sexual conno-
tation, which became stronger when I heard about his theory
of the Oedipus complex. I got mad at my father sometimes,
but *kill* him? And sleep with . . . my *mother*? Yikes! What an
unappetizing idea! But didn't everyone say that Freud was a
great genius? It was very confusing, this Oedipus complex.
Better to think about his ideas on the interpretation of dreams
and his amusing examples of slips of the tongue. I liked the
Latin term for it, *lapsus linguae*. I knew that the first word was
in the nominative case and the second the genitive. But wait,
genitive was close to *genital*. Ah, no escape!

Another Thing That Annoys Me

The spelling of *40*. We have *four* and *fourteen*, and then, for no reason I know of, the *u* is dropped and we're left with *forty*, not to mention the schizophrenic *forty-four*. Most annoying, as Sei Shōnagon would say.

Over There

I have always assumed that my body would provide
reliable transportation to carry me through the day
and no I will not extend that metaphor
and if you know what that means
you'll know what I mean.

John Ashbery once said
"I never get up before the crack of noon."
Pope Francis said
"I am Argentinian. You know
how an Argentinian commits suicide?
He climbs up on top of his ego and jumps off."
"That's all, Bruno,"
Fairfield Porter said to his dog.
Does it help to know that Bruno was a golden retriever?
And that Fairfield was invisible?
All of a sudden.

Agreement

I was
You were
He, she, it was

Wait a minute

Why shouldn't *you*
also be followed by *was?*

If I were you
I'd say "was"

But I wasn't you
I never was
nor will I ever be

In class we chuckled
when we recited
"He, *she-it* is"

and the masculine came first
except when going through a door

Then the word *she*
went through a door

and into a new world

You wasn't there

You were "he"
and it kept being "it"

but don't blame "it"

"It" doesn't even know it's there

The Space Heater

The electric heater—
a cylindrical column
about a yard high
with a silver grille on one side
and behind it two vertical rods
that glow a rich orange—
looks like a ray gun
in an old science-fiction film,
the kind a hero would have aimed
at alien invaders and—*zap!*
Buck Rogers was his name,
leaping heroism was his game,
while his cousin Roy made sure
the West was grand and pure,
his six-gun at his side.
Something about it makes me
want to scream, as if
I had touched an electric heater
on at full blast.

The Great Divide

Excellent thrill-waves flood my head
like steam rising from lust
that has become intellectual.
And then you went into the eighth grade,
where the light hurt your feelings
and killing is immoral—
you have just killed yourself,
in a way. So go sit
in the pink traveling jail and brood,
for the girl who glints like a wink in a mirror
is still chewing her gum and looking around
as if everything is a little bit funny.

Philosophy

Think of it as a description of events and actions
rather than an exposition of ideas and substances

though of course ideas are events too
and ideas are what we make of them.

Thus ends my disquisition. I will now
step down and take my place

among the cobblers and their shoes—
if one can call them that, scraps

of leather bound with thongs every
which way. My shoes are nicer

because I live in a later period
in which footwear is said to be

advanced. But what about Mercury
and those little wings on his feet?

Of what substance were they made?
And by whose idea? And when he flew

what was the philosophy
that let him fly?

Start

Each time I do just the thought of you
Makes me stop before I begin
— *Cole Porter*

I want to do something, but I don't know what. Save my country? Of course, but that's impossible. Be young, or at least forget about my decrepit, sick, and dying friends? That sounds good, the being young part. Sell all my possessions and go live in a . . . what? An igloo?

I've never quite accepted the idea that human beings live or lived in igloos. Since childhood I've thought that the last place I'd want to be in a severely cold climate is inside a hut made of—of all things!—ice. Okay, let's assume there were no materials with which to build a warmer shelter. But why didn't they migrate south, where they could find some trees or mud? Why did the Eskimo man arrive on a sheet of ice and say to his female companion, "Honey, this looks like a good place to settle down"?

In 1967 I arrived in a trashed apartment in a slum and said to my wife, "Honey, this looks like a good place to live." She was not an Eskimo, but she grunted and went to work cleaning the kitchen.

But I'm not interested in the past, I'm just mildly obsessed with it, fearing that if I let go of it I will float off into some endless psychic space. And besides, how much of a future could there be, and who would "I" be in it? A sack of bones being shifted in a nursing-home bed? (But listening to Bach!) Or perhaps an old gent being helped off an airliner by an attractive young woman provided by the Ministry of Culture, on my way to give a reading of my poems on French national television? But am I supposed to read them in French or in English? It's a moot point, because I have lost the satchel that contained the poems, left it . . . where? Perhaps I can phone the airport or the taxi company in New York. But I don't have a telephone, and the young woman . . . where is she? She has gone back to China, to the land of her birth, where her village awaits her, in the year 1736, cook smoke rising from the huts and thinning out into the evening air.

It's like what I was saying to an old friend today: "Many writers our age wish they had been in Paris in the early part of the twentieth century, and some younger writers today wish they had been in New York in the 1960s, and the really young ones wish they had been here in the 1990s! The measurement keeps sliding forward." It would be wonderful to . . . I was about to say wonderful to find oneself walking down the street in ancient Athens (*"Kalimera,* Socrates!") but I chastised myself for having this banal thought, and then I realized that what was *not* banal was the full vision I had of momentarily being there among those strange creatures, the Athenians, for that one hallucinatory moment, and how it happened so quickly that I didn't have time to be terrified by its otherness.

A few years before my grandmother (1900–1998) died she told me how clearly she recalled being eight years old, atop a horse and wearing a pretty dress with blue ribbons, riding from the farm into town (Springdale, Arkansas) on a nice Saturday morning, and as she said this I wished I had been the horse or a tree or the road so that I could have been in that moment with her, so beautiful it was.

"Return with us now to those thrilling days of yesteryear!" intoned the voice of the man who led us into another episode of the adventures of that peculiar cowboy, the Lone Ranger, who, it turned out, was not so lone, being accompanied by his faithful sidekick, Tonto. We do not know that *tonto* in Spanish means *stupid,* so we are innocently swept into the black-and-white world on the screen, a world of dust and sunlight and decent, hardworking homesteaders rescued from brutality and injustice by the Lone Ranger, who asks nothing in return, who

in fact at the end simply rides off into the distance, going . . .
where? To his next adventure, perhaps. Certainly not to lie
down and sleep or do anything else ordinary, such as laun-
der his mask. And though the people he saved always wonder,
"Who was that masked man?" we do not share their curios-
ity, for we know that he is the Lone Ranger, and that explains
everything.

I would like to be in Paris with the Lone Ranger, walking
down the boulevard Saint-Germain in 1920, even though pass-
ersby might think he is the clever archcriminal Fantômas in a
cowboy costume, but the Lone Ranger and Fantômas no lon-
ger exist the way they once did, just like the boulevard and
all of Paris itself. Every time I return to that beautiful city I
walk down the streets I knew fifty-two years ago, searching for
them, even though they are there, but what I am looking for
is the feeling of being in those streets back then, and of course
that feeling is long gone, as if it too wore a mask and had dis-
appeared over the horizon in a cloud of dust.

Flying Down to Up There

A thought in a brain and *uno,*
there, whale, here, whaleness:
footprints across the top of the world
where I genuflect to the phone
and say hello to South America—
I think it is going to blow up
like a saint who flies not
to make a point but *to* an appointment
with the arriving rays that turn
you into a burning bird whose song
freezes even firemen in their aureoles,
arms and wings of pomp and flame
whiplashed into place.

Geometry of the Sandwich

If you make a sandwich
using two pieces of traditional American sandwich bread
and slice it diagonally
you end up with two right triangles.
Well, technically one of them is not a triangle,
since where its right angle should be
is rounded.
Look at the sandwich:
the two halves look different.

The difference is a very small thing to notice,
so small as to be useless
in the great rush of life.
I feel sorry for its smallness.

Bubble

It's a very great pleasure
to walk with you in November,
our bodies sleepy in the clarity
falling across the city
and to feel a kiss arrive
from a height of five feet two
and new shadows on my shirt
rising and falling as I live
and breathe with you.

Free at Last

There must have been
some magic in
that old silk hat
they found,
for when they placed it
on his head
he began
to dance around,
he being God,
the Christian God
who in the Bible
was so grumpy
and now
is without a care
in the world.

At Benny the Bungalow

Once upon a time there was a bungalow named Benny. Inside the bungalow were two chairs, each with a little table next to it.

On one table was a vase of red flowers. On the other table was a brown paper bag.

Rabbit and her little boy, Clyde, knocked on the door of the bungalow, then they chuckled and went on in. It was their bungalow!

Rabbit picked up the vase of red flowers and sniffed them, sighing, "Ahhh!"

Clyde reached into the brown paper bag and pulled out a magic wand and a sandwich. The sandwich started to grow bigger and bigger, but when he tapped it with the wand it shrank back to its normal size. Then he took a bite and munched.

There were two knocks at the door. Rabbit and Clyde went over and looked out the window.

Outside were two people who looked exactly like Rabbit and Clyde. Neither pair could tell whether they were looking through a window or into a mirror. But this was the kind of thing that happened at Benny the Bungalow. It happened all the time.

The Sunny Side of the Street

I will never stop being surprised
by the great number of words
in the English language whose exact
nuances and histories I still don't know.
Meanwhile the sunlight is happily battering
the facade of the building across the street
I see through the window and whose windows
look back and see me here
with a little bit of their sunlight
on my suddenly old right arm, and my head
the one big puzzlement it's been all my life
though all along I thought it knew something
it would tell me someday and
all I get is sunlight coming across the street,
but it's better than, say, pitchforks.

I'll Get It

1.

It's quite satisfying
to have a key ring
with a bunch of keys on it
and to pick the right one
and put it in a lock
and turn it till
it goes *click*.

Locking *up*
is *clunk*.

2.

Yesterday my mother
would have been 96,
but she wasn't.
I tried to get her there
but she wouldn't budge.
She's stuck at 75,
younger than me.

3.

I've arranged the books by genre
but now I also have the urge
to put labels on the shelves:
Poetry, Fiction, Etc.,
"Etc." for those books
that leap down off the shelves
because they don't want to be
in a category.
I jump up and jump
around the room,
boing! boing! boing!
but I can't catch them.

4.

Walking across the lawn
I was trapped
in the figure of a man
walking across the lawn
and I couldn't get out
and in some funny way
I didn't want to,
though being a human
is probably not the best
thing to be. What is?
You know, everything.

5.

There's a portrait of a Chinese emperor
who looks ugly,
I mean *really* ugly,
in fact so ugly
that all I can think is
that in his day
he *wasn't* considered ugly
or else the artist
would have been chopped up
and fed to the royal pigs.
"Emperor!" they squeal,
"Give us the artist!"
But he will not,
for the portrait has made him
handsome for all time.

6.

At sixteen
I decided to be a poet
forever
and now, sixty-one years later,
I stop writing
and slap my ear,
but the wily mosquito
zooms off in a blur of sound.
At birth he was a mosquito
but in a day or two
he'll wish he had been a poet,
even one like me,
ear throbbing.

7.

I like the way the hair
on the back of my hand looks
when it's gold against tan skin,
but when it's brown against white
it looks ugly as sin,
when sin is ugly,
which it always is,
according to some people.
"As *beautiful* as sin"
would wreck our moral system,
or what's left of it.
I guess we'd better
leave that alone, as is, alas.

8.

Remember those motorcycle daredevils
who rode on the walls
on the inside of a drum
fifty feet in diameter,
parallel to the ground?
You don't?
Well, okay.

9.

The phone rang
and I called out
"*I'll* get it!"
but there was no one
in the house
except me.
I saved my wife
from answering the phone
though she wasn't there.
That's how much
I love her
or am a nut.

10.

In tai chi class
someone mentioned
Taoist tai chi
and I thought
"Ooo, that sounds *really* good."
This is the thought of someone
who needs to lie down
like one hundred people
in the high mountains,
where the air is all mirth.

11.

The view through
my window never
looked like this—
red, orange, and
light-green leaves
jumping in random
jumps as raindrops
spatter them one
at a time,
all of it
blocking the view
up the path
into the woods,
like the ringing
in my ears
I didn't notice
until just now.

12.

In the 1,136 pages of *War and Peace*
there is only one comic passage,
late in the book, when Tolstoy
summarizes the Napoleonic Wars:
"He conquered everyone everywhere, that is, he killed a great
many people, because he was a very great genius. And for some
reason he went to kill the Africans; and killed them so well,
and was so cunning and clever, that on returning to France
he bade everyone obey him. And they all did obey him. After
being made Emperor he went to kill people in Italy, Austria,
and Prussia. And there he killed a great many."
The passage continues in this vein,
like writing in a children's book,
then switches back to serious.
What made him use this comic tone?
Napoleon wasn't funny. He was horrible.
And the French erected a huge monument
to house his coffin, inside of which
they placed that little piece of shit.

13.

The asters wave their heads and say
"Sorry to be so late, but
we got held up by the weather,
which caused a big traffic jam,
all those daffodils, peonies, and day lilies
ahead of us, just lolling around
and taking up space."

We cut them and bring them inside
and put them in a vase,
and they just stand there
like startled exclamation points
whose heads are exploding,
as if they were flowers.

14.

Lee Crabtree came to my apartment
and sat on the floor.
He said he didn't need a chair.
We talked about what? and then
he gave me the sheet music
for a song he said we wrote.
Then he left.
The next I heard
he waved to someone
straight across from him,
high in an office window,
and jumped. What,
forty years ago?
It's hard to believe
this isn't a story
I made up.
Lee just jumped.

Close Enough

When I told the poet from South Africa
that when de Kooning came to see Frank
in the hospital, Frank all battered and purple
and covered with tubes, Frank opened his eyes
and said, "Oh, Bill, you shouldn't have gone
to the trouble," her eyes filled with tears,
though she didn't know much
of anything about Frank O'Hara's life.
[I didn't think to tell her that he too
could get emotional—ballet could
make him cry or a movie or one drink
too many and a friend to cry with.]
Let's put that in brackets so I can remember
to cut it out the next time I see it. And
now my ankle itches, the cool morning
is flowing into the many windows of this room,
borne by birdsong and the light of the sun
that has come all this way just to help us
find our way around and recognize each other
from the distance we keep until we forget to
and become a part of the perfect space we're in
because we let ourselves just be there. Like Frank
and Bill? Not exactly, but close enough.

The World without John Ashbery

The world without John Ashbery
has lasted for one day
so far. Soon
one week, one century.
Will people look back
and scratch their heads
the way some do now?
I hope not. But
it's out of my hands
anyway, and I
won't care one whit.
But what he did,
his poetry, that is,
is great.
He gave me a conjunction
and I ran away with it,
though it kept turning
me around, so I ran back.
And here I am
with a conjunction
on my hands.
My idea
was to give it back,
but instead
I'm going to move
the forest six inches
to the left and leave it
at that.

Bill Berkson's Obituary

Two weeks ago you and I
walked down First Avenue
a few blocks before good-bye,
and now I'm walking the same way
with the *Times* tucked under my arm
while you go on out into the whole world
like the perfect gentleman
you always will be,
true and loyal friend.
I'll open the paper at home,
not till then.

Sleepyhead

It's hard to describe
how falling asleep I am,
clouds rising around me pink and blue
and I a dot.

The Dream of the Cadillac

I dreamed I was me
writing this poem

and then I was

When I was a child
people in movies
who got shot in the back
always died

So when the bad guy said
"Turn around"
you'd better not do it

There is no such thing as a poem
Only this poem exists

Or that one
and the bullet flew

Becoming human
must have been terrifying
so they found things
to distract them
They dreamed they were they

in a Cadillac

There is only one Cadillac
in the world
The others are dreams of Cadillacs

I saw the water
but could not make it be
anything else

The glass was neither half full
nor half empty the glass
was not there yet

Like how morning is just around the corner
but you can't see it it's
still dark
though you can hear the Cadillac in it
the engine running
the Cadillac not moving

until the dim edge of the corner appears
in the dawn
and everything gets to be there for a moment
before it's there

Elephant Walk

Once when I was asleep
someone tapped me on the shoulder
and a jolt of cold fear went through me
until I saw it was my own finger.
I was relieved
it wasn't some nut
who had gotten into my bedroom
and decided to tap me on the shoulder.

There was a movie about elephants
that rampaged through the jungle,
knocking everything down—I think
it was called *Elephant Walk*.
I don't recall why they wanted
to knock everything down, they
just seemed very unhappy.

There was another movie
in which a tidal wave of voracious ants
came buzz-cutting their way through the jungle,
chewing up everything in their path,
and the hero had to figure out
what to do, as his girlfriend
kept jerking her hands
to the sides of her head in terror.
I remember thinking that the ants
were going to chew off his and her legs
if they didn't get out of there fast, go
to a different continent where the ants weren't so hungry.
I wanted to tap him on the shoulder.

Big Anniversary

It's October 9th,
a day that means nothing
to me. I can't think
of a single thing associated
with it, no birthday
or disaster, no holiday
or date of death.
It will be replaced
by October 10th, another day
with no resonance
other than the resonance of everything,
which, come to think of it,
is a lot.

The Waiting Room

What are you waiting for?
You almost know
what it is,
but still you wait
in a space in which
you think you'll hold back time,
but time has a way
of getting its way,
and there you are,
left behind with your illusion,
in which you wait
for it to disappear
the way Casper the Friendly Ghost did,
though he's waiting for you,
turning the pages of the comic book
you are still reading.

Wait

A second. I mean
a minute. Then a day
or two. Longer,
like years. There
grows a tree
in paradise
and children say things.
What do they know,
those adorable little morons?

Edge Puppet

The puppet dances
all this way and that,
loose-jointed, head
flopping side to side,
in his commedia dell'arte costume,
a song in his heart,
and he is happy to be there
on the outskirts of town,
dancing like a puppet
with tears in his eyes
that see the tears from inside,
where he is pulling his own strings.

Pencils and Pens

Every once in a while when I open my desk drawer, the flat, shallow one right in front of me, my eyes send to my brain the information that the numerous pens and pencils I had arranged so neatly have once again become strewn this way and that, in jumbles and piles crisscrossing the other items in the drawer—erasers, paper-clip boxes, rubber bands, a staple box, a box of small screwdrivers, two pocketknives, a flashlight, picture wire, tape, small screws, a padlock, a shoehorn, three pairs of scissors, two old wristwatches, a staple puller, map tacks, a hole punch, address labels, a photographer's loupe, postage stamps, a bottle of ink, rubber stamps, rubber stamp pads, batteries, a tape measure, and rulers—and I am seized with the desire to sort the pens and pencils into categories and place them in appropriate areas in the drawer again, but today this desire was shunted aside by the sudden realization that the words that might issue from these instruments will never flow forth from most of them, that whatever I might have said with them will remain forever locked inside them, and that I, as a physical body, am a kind of pencil or pen from which whatever I might say will never issue. A sad thought! But then, when you think about it, not so much sad as normal, at least as measured against the behavior of most of humanity, for don't people rarely express the range of what they think or feel?

Many years ago I described myself as a pencil, but I did it only because I liked the word *pencil* itself—the way it looks and sounds—not because I was using it metaphorically. It is too commonplace a metaphor to arouse any interest in me, but today when I stared into my desk drawer and saw the chaos of pencils and pens, the metaphor became uncontrollable and explosive, and I could not count the explosions, and for a moment I felt afraid. Then the urge to rearrange the pens and pencils drove out my fear, allowing me to anticipate the satisfaction of accomplishing something that is so unimportant as to be almost pointless.

Esther's Notebook

On the reverse side of the page that carries *Les Cahiers d'Esther*—these days the only comic strip I read—are real-estate ads that remind me of the life I was never able to give my wife. Here's one for a cream-colored house in Paris in the seventh arrondissement, in its own private alley off the rue de Grenelle, an eighteenth-century gem with thirteen rooms (six bedrooms) on four levels, near shops and excellent schools—the kind of property that rarely comes onto the market. About six million dollars. And a private parking area. On the reverse side of the page Esther is thirteen, learning how to deal with the world.

Reality

Nature is everywhere the same,
In Paris and in Terre Haute.
Dombasle's Triptolemus by another name.
A chlamys is a petticoat.

La Vallière in her coach,
Fancying Mars or the Roi Soleil,
Was as ferocious
As Aphrodite in her shell.

O sons and brothers, O poets,
When a thing is, say it's so.
Be of spirit pure, and then do it.
When the soul is high, nothing's low.

A hiccup escapes Silenus
Among the roses of Paestum.
When Horace gives us Priapus,
Shakespeare may risk Bottom.

Truth has no bounds.
Thanks to bestial Pan, the real
Shows its godly horns
On the blue forehead of the ideal.

—*Victor Hugo*

Apostrophe

To myself

One common error is the misuse of the apostrophe in *its* (or *it's*). Example: The tournament is in it's fifth year.

Now the clatter of pick-up sticks. If small children can learn to play pick-up sticks, surely they can learn how to use the apostrophe, which is, after all, only one stick. Yes, it has two sides, one for forming possessives and one for indicating dropped letters, and it has two edges, one for confusing you and one for confusing you even more.

Not that confusion is all bad. Sometimes I propel myself into the kitchen not sure whether I want coffee or not. The very fact that it doesn't matter and that I am standing there like an apostrophe in the morning light gives me a thrill. Its my thrill. It's my thrill.

Flash Cards

My second-grade teacher would hold up a card with 2 + 2 or
some other math problem on it. The first student who called
out the correct answer got to take that card. When she had
gone through the entire set, the student with the most cards
got to take her place, but there was no point in keeping score,
since I always won them all. Vain as I was, I couldn't decide
whether it was better to be at my seat winning or at the front
flashing the cards. It was a few steps from my desk to the front.
Since those days, I have been able to take only a few steps away
from myself, and when I turn around I can bear only a quick
peek between my fingers.

The Uprising of the Beans

The baked beans fly into the living room
where Mom, Dad, and Sis
are locked in a mah-jongg tussle.
Dad is soon covered with beans
that bang against his body, crying
"We want *something*!
We demand *something*!"
"Little beans," he says,
"you can have anything
you want," and the beans
cheer and dance as Mom and Sis
swing into radiant harmony.
Dad is great.

Love Song

It is drifting, the season, it
is bent, like a racetrack

and the memory of you with white lace collar
and black dress bent back, the top part

of you grazing the top part of me
and the rest of you swept into the dark.

Coffee Corner

The large bowls of coffee at breakfast in old France,
the heavy porcelain cups in old American diners,
the brown plastic cups in cheap motel lobbies,

the feeling that you ought to drink the entire cup,
the slight resentment you feel at feeling this,
the wondering why you do it then, you dope,

the gratitude for someone's making the coffee,
the decision not to have a third free refill,
the surprise of a really bad cup of coffee,

the way it used to cost a nickel, then a dime,
and now anywhere up to god knows what
(you brought your credit card, right?),

the brown print drying on the lip of the cup,
the trace left in the bottom,
the rest of it thrumming inside you,

thrumming its stimulation through tubes
in your body, hello, let's go, are we late, do
you have the keys, oh god I can't find my wallet.

Shadows at Noon

One of my college professors told me that when comparing two things (as in "He's as big as a house"), the first *as* should be *so* when following a negative verb ("He's not so big as a house"). Because I respected my teacher, I unhesitatingly accepted this rule, but I have never found it in any grammar manual, so in defending it to others I have had no recourse other than to say "It's what F. W. Dupee told me." One weakness of this defense is that few people now know who he was. He left behind only one collection of essays and a diminishing number of students who might still remember this fine point of his exactitude.

My term paper for his Modern Poetry course discussed what happened at noon in the poetry of Emily Dickinson.

In 1965, one year after college, I found myself living in Paris. One day, in a small shop on the rue Mazarine, I bought a used book called *Ombres chinoises,* a title much more intriguing than its English translation (*Shadow Puppets*). The book focused on the shadow-puppet plays performed in the late nineteenth century at Le Chat Noir, the Montmartre cabaret where other acts included Erik Satie at the piano and a fellow known as Le Pétomane, who was able to blow out a candle by farting. I became so fascinated by shadow-puppet plays that I decided to write a book about their history, apparently something no one had ever done. In the following years I took notes for this endeavor, which I kept in a manila file folder, but the project remained there, a few scraps of paper.

Who

Who is that knocking at my chamber door?
Who is that whose foot is standing on the floor?

It is me mum, come to say one word:
"Ron" in a tone no one can understand

for it is not a name, it is a power
that drove her life up to a point and then

off. The boy at fifty-eight who held her hand
and felt that final squeeze, so strong

for one so near to death, now sits
and puts his Ron foot on the floor.

F

I'm thinking in my sleep about the word *fetal* because I realize that's the position my arms are in, and then the variant spelling *foetal* clicks into place. Was the initial *f* a modernization of *ph*? Or do all *f* words come from Latin and all *ph* words from Greek? *Fantastic* and *phenomenal*—these words start to whirl around, both inside my head and outside my body, then they fly up onto a distant hilltop that is backlit by the sun that will soon rise. I uncurl my arms.

Soft Roll

Last night my wife
bit into a soft roll
and her tooth fell out
just like that,
no warning, no pain,
no nothing and now
no tooth, except
the one she held
in the palm of her hand
as she said
"I'm falling apart"
and laughed.

People Take Pictures of Each Other

You think of the people
you used to know,
relatives and close friends,
and how they got reduced
and sucked onto photographic paper,
living on in a black-and-white world,
which isn't so bad for them
while you're thinking of them,
but when you aren't
they have to stop and wait
for you to bring your mind
back to them
and then they are happy,
almost laughing.

Pipe Dream

1.

I yearned to find the love of my life, never certain that I *would* find her and that someday I would wake up at 5 a.m., fix toast and tea, and realize that without her I am nothing. Before her I was something—a young man yearning for her—and now I'm an old man yearning for her, for me.

2.

There is no song lyric more moving than "September Song": "And these few precious days I'll spend with you." *Moving* is not the right word, it's more like *gut-wrenching* or *heart-stabbing*—a physical assault. The words fly toward me, but I bat them away and wait for my next breath.

3.

It's the next day and the same raindrops are going *tap-tap-tappity-tap* on my roof, but the idea of a bluebird has landed on my shoulder ever so gently. I have no fear that it will peck me or dig its claws into my flesh, for it is a serene bluebird, even more exalted than the bluebird of happiness. On the other shoulder is an unoccupied space—not even air is there—open for the arrival of something tremendous, such as a smattering of periods in search of sentences to end.

4.

5.

I've never been able to understand an experience I'm in. It's all too everything. That is, a *now-or-never* whose *now* disappears and whose *never* seems forever. I guess that that clarification doesn't help. Let me try it this way: childhood, I had no idea; adolescence, no idea; adulthood, ditto; and now, total ditto. But sometimes—not often—there comes the feeling that everything is all right anyway, that the pipe is having a dream about *you*.

Falling Asleep in Poetry

It's hard to write a poem
when you are on the verge
of falling asleep, but Robert
Desnos could do it, even when
he *was* asleep, or so
the story goes.
There are photos of him
lying on a couch asleep,
but is he writing a poem?
I don't remember any utensils.
Just his heavy eyelids.

"You are standing on my eyelids"
wrote his fellow poet Paul Éluard,
"you" being not Desnos but a woman.
It feels like neither poet
had to work hard
to write their poems,
even Desnos when awake.
I thought writing this poem would wake me up,
but it woke him up instead,
and Éluard has tiptoed away.

In Conclusion

I've come to the conclusion
that humanity is hopelessly stupid,
even more stupid than a raindrop,
but that if we could achieve the intelligence of a raindrop
we would be happy
to be one
and go splat.

Pants

Good morning, pants
of Nature, blue striding
across my visual field,
a hearty hello to you
and a thank-you for striding,
even if you are just a bug
making tiny waves on a pond.
You are still the pants of Nature!

Lunch Bucket

How corny and sentimental
it is to remember the lunch bucket
my grandfather took to work,
black metal with a vaulted lid
hinged to the rectangular box
inside of which was a thermos of coffee
and a sandwich and maybe
a hard-boiled egg. He himself
was anything but hard-boiled,
just a regular guy
though kinder than most
and gentler.
I see him in the big metal shed,
among the metal pipes and grinders,
with a dim light filtering in
as he sits down next to Gomez,
the new guy some people called a "wetback,"
whose English made my grandpa laugh,
and opens the lunch box,
unscrews the plastic thermos cap,
and pours the coffee into it.
He was glad to have a job
and he liked Gomez.

Otter Moment

I just saw an otter,
at first a head moving
just above the surface,
then disappearing underwater
for a while and coming up
near the bank, forelegs pulling him
up onto it, and undulating
across the ground, a shining
and oh dear unattractive
fat tube. In *his* world
he's gorgeous!

Parallel Parallels

Two parallel lines
have two *l*'s in their name
but want to be perpendicular
to each other.
Don't they have anything better to do?
Off they go
into an area called Zen,
where they are welcomed,
the first parallel lines
in Zen!
With an exclamation point
perpendicular to them!

Peppermint Air

Only twenty minutes and
I already don't smell
the peppermint oil
on the cotton balls
I have placed in this room
to keep the mice out.
I sit here in a cube of air,
a big nonmouse.

Ping

The time will come
when the car will stop
and you will get out,
the car will go on
and you will see
all around you
nothing,
absolutely nothing,
then *ping*

Knockouts

Ça a l'air de rimer
—*Apollinaire*

Do you speak English?
I don't speak Russian.
I am a great poet.
I am a great tennis player.
Where is the bathroom?

The Chinese word for *something*
is *tongshi,*
made up of two characters,
tong (west) and *shi* (east).
That seems to make sense.

When you scratch your head
your fingers curl up
like a question mark.

So he said, "Let's run
and have some fun before I melt away."
Without legs, run?

Like Birnam Wood
to Dunsinane, eh?

That seems to rhyme, eh?

Long ago
I made the mistake of thinking
that life is mysterious.
Life is not mysterious.

It is mysterious
only to those
who think about it too much.
Peasants don't think
that life is mysterious.
They are too busy staying alive.

There is some word
that feels like it should have a *j* in it
but I can't remember what it is

Not *picaresque*

(as in *Don Quixote*)

or *babushka*

A monkey jumped on a buzzard's back

sticks spinning in the air
like "evil"

and that movie theater
in Paris, what was it—
"oriental"
like a cross
between a xylophone and a pyramid
and on the rue de Grenelle, wasn't it?
I lay in bed
in its green jade embrace.

La Pagode!

of course—rue de Babylone

Look, I can't do anything
about it, it being like
Nevada or vanishing

and let the Devil take tomorrow

for it doesn't matter
what you think
but why you think it

and it took me a while
but now I'm inside your face
and I won't leave until I
feel like it, friend,
and I don't mind
giving you the creeps—
in fact,
I kind of like
being made of snow

A young woman
with pink hair
starts across the street
as if she were someone else,
the hair very so what,
but it rides across the street,
a pink cloud
on its own,
so not so so-what.
Electricity

is like the nervous system,
branching and buzzing
inside that pink hair
that is still riding

inside my pink head.
I am a pink snowman.
You don't believe me,
because you don't have pink anything.

In Syria some children
have red hair, red
with blood, that is.
Let's put them all
in a box and fold it
so it vanishes,
like they just did.
Boom boom boom boom,
as the song says.
You knocks me out.
Like Nevada.

So when I wake up
the first thing I do
is nothing.
I just lie there
saturated with myself.
Then I knock myself out
and from all over my body
little points of light
float out into the room.
Boom boom boom boom.

My Early Childhood

My name was Ronnie
and I knew it,
though I had four black lines
that formed a box around me,
not too close, and there
were wiggling lines
emanating from each
of those four black lines,
wiggling and waving
as if craziness lived inside them,
and the great thing
is that I had no idea
they were there.
After all,
they weren't hurting anybody.

In Umbria

Because I have no hope of ever going back
—*Guido Cavalcanti*

So how *did* Perugino get from Perugia to Florence?
On a donkey?
And who went with him?
Oho!
Here are raindrops falling from the sky
onto his head and shoulders,
and the ears and the mane of his donkey have drops too
because that's what happens
when you can't buy an umbrella on the corner
from the little old Chinese woman
whose ancestors made a screen
that shows us winding our way
through the hills in the now slanting rain.

Pluto

If you have ever wondered what
it's like to be human,
keep wondering, brothers
and sisters, because that's all
you can do
to try to catch
in your hands
whatever it is
that moves away
when you reach for it.
Pluto used to be a planet
and a dog, now
it's a what?

Russian Mountain

I said, "What does *montaña* mean?"
and the kids shouted, "Mountain!"
"Aha. So what does *rusa* mean?"
"Russian!"
"So *montaña rusa* means *Russian mountain*."
"No!" they laughed.
"What does it mean?"
"Roller coaster, you know, like
the Cyclone at Coney Island."
I didn't tell them
I knew that all along.
They were so happy
on Russian Mountain.

Ticket

A car drives through
the visual patterns
in my brain, the driver
my father
totally at ease
at 110 miles per hour.
All I see
is a blur go by
but I know who
it is.

Both of Me

Paul, the Separated Man / Leaped forward
—Kenneth Koch

The reasonable part of me knows that the song title "Who Can
I Turn To?" would not sound so good if it were "Whom Can I
Turn To?" and the pedantic part feels that the more grammati-
cally correct *whom* should be kept alive, to slow its slippage
into desuetude, becoming more of a marker of one's education
than a useful, if small, tool for communicating well, for I tend
to forget that there is room enough in the world for both the
formally correct and the colloquial, and that in any case there
is nothing I can do to change the course of the history of our
language. It is what it is.

In high-school French class, first year, our teacher intro-
duced the rules for the agreement of nouns and adjectives.
For example, *cher monsieur* became, when addressing a mature
or married woman, *chère madame.* One student raised his
hand and asked a perfectly sincere question: "Why don't they
just keep *cher* the same, the way we do with *dear sir* and *dear
madam?*" The teacher looked at him for a moment and then
delivered a crushing truth: "Because they don't."

I don't think she went on to say that although we can trace
the changes of a language throughout history, we can't always
explain *why* things developed the way they did, and in this
case *why* isn't a useful question to raise, because knowing the
answer won't make us learn French any faster. She might have
pointed out that English has its own puzzlements, and that a
language such as Chinese, which Westerners tend to think of
as hopelessly complicated, is grammatically much simpler than
English, as it has no singular or plural nouns, no agreement

of nouns and adjectives, no agreement of subject and verb, no articles, and no past or future tense, at least as we conceive of them, but I doubt that she knew much about Chinese, and besides it probably would not have made the student feel less perplexed. No, when it comes to a language, it is what it is, just as the student was who he was. (Bob Stubblefield.)

Which, believe it or not, brings me to matches. My childish assumption was that they are called that because they look identical. If you spill a box of them onto a table, you cannot tell one from the other, a fact that doesn't worry you, as they look rather beautiful spilled out like that. A few days ago someone asked me about the matches in a poem of mine: perhaps I had written about them because, although rather insignificant objects, they represent reality? My immediate thought was to answer no and let it go at that, but instead I agreed that a match could be an example of reality, as indeed anything can, and that a match has as much reality as a mountain. Of course a match doesn't "have" reality, it is an example of reality, or at least what we commonly refer to as reality. Then it turned out that the word *match* does not derive from similarity of appearance, but rather from an ancient Greek word.

Alex Katz painted a portrait of Allen Ginsberg on six separate aluminum sheets of different sizes and shapes, on each of which is a section of Ginsberg's face—frontal, turned slightly, and in profile—in varying degrees of close-up. Four of the pieces are mounted on a wall and the other two are freestanding in front of them, about four feet from the wall, forming what might be called a highly controlled and frozen cubistic explosion. Faced simultaneously with one fragment zoomed in and another zoomed out, I felt as if I had gotten inside Ginsberg's face! It's like walking down a busy street in Manhattan and realizing that you're actually *in* the street that's *out* there. That is, not only are you alive, you *are* life, and who you are seems, for a moment at least, beside whatever the point might be.

Visible Ink

This is the room
where many years ago
I'd lock myself in
and then lock myself
into myself.
It was as safe
as being in
an invisible safe
and all I had to do
was wait
for the words
that leaped
into my . . . what?
and slid down
inside my pen
and onto where
the paper was.

But now when I walk
into that room I bang
my head on the edge
of the door and blood
falls from my forehead
onto the floor
in a pool
that gets redder
and redder.
I'm surprised
you don't see it.

Encore with Rectangle and Philosophy

> I built a house / and had ideas in it.
> —*Ron Padgett*

Initio it was weird,
everything,
Boom!
ribbons and shimmering everywhere,
and this and thisness:
stop, look, and sound too
waiting to come out
as soon as movement said to,
and a bone walked around
as if something had happened to it,
like, an infinity ago.

• • •

Excuse me.
I have to get up
and walk around a little.
My abode
is dark and cozy
but sometimes it turns me
into a bowling ball,
and yes
I weigh sixteen pounds
and am suddenly marbleized
as I hook into the pocket
and decimate all ten pins
in one explosive explosion!
—Wait, *decimate*
is not the *mot juste,*

nor *cave* nor *bowling ball.*
(My soul has just multiplied itself,
in case.)

On second thought,
I don't think
I *can* get up.
Would you give me a hand?
Shakespeare?

What is Shakespeare?
The fellow bound
upon a wheel of fire
and rolled up into the sky?

• • •

I'm stuck to a moment,
then it goes away.

I am not stuck to the world,
I *am* the world,
two feet tall
and zero deep and wide.
Look at the picture
in the dictionary
next to the word *mysticism:*
there's nothing there.
What do you think about
that?
(You're coming out of the wrong side of my head.)

• • •

Pronouns aren't for everybody.

• • •

My head went into everybody
the way vowels went into words
and life was a little easier,
then,
the way the Pacific Ocean
was easier than the Atlantic
and *best* was better than *better,*
and the barnyard swung open
in a kind of orchestral majesty
that got sucked into a pile of cow dung,
which caused ancient China to wake up
and be modern China, smiling
and gesturing Oh hello! and everything.
I gave the driver some yuan
and got out of the taxi inwardly,
and then got out outwardly,
the driver went forward
into a pile of cow dung.
I figured there was time,
but for what?
Everybody went into my head
the way harmony went into music.

• • •

There are a lot of details in the world
—too many for me, so
I *blur* them, using my ability to *blur,*
except now instead of you
I see invisible ink and it's thrilling
in a different way (for me,
not for you).

•••

In the middle
of the night
What
is the name of that island
we went to
way back when and what
should be done with my ashes?
It had two pronunciations,
one for its citizens, one
for the rest of us. Released
into the stream in Vermont, perhaps.

Aside from the Hague,
how many cities begin (in English)
with *the*?

•••

Antigua.
I wrote it down.

•••

If you think
about the tasks
ahead of you
in the day,
go ahead and turn them
into small rectangles,
sweep them
into your hand
and toss them outside.
Then kill yourself.

• • •

The Bronx.
I wrote it up.

• • •

Beating so.
You give your hand to me
and then you say hello,
but I can hardly speak
my heart is . . .

. . . like the fork *now*
falling toward the floor and everything
falling as you grab grab grab

• • •

O my.
That's what people used to say.
God had left the sentence.
O me.

• • •

Coleridge
sat alone under a lime tree,
missing his friends,
and wrote about it—
a bird flew past,
electrifying,
the first time that something happened
during the writing of a poem
and got included.

Okay, first a bat goes by
and then a bee is singing,
and then the bird (a rook)
"(Now a dim speck, now vanishing in light)."
The bat and the bee I forget
but that bird is bang on.

• • •

The idea of 1/3
is more appealing
than the idea of 2/3.

• • •

I built a house
that had ideas in it.
Am I supposed to be
the something of something?

• • •

It's a long way
between love of country
and licking your lips.
You're told to love your country
by people who want you
to obey them but never tell you
that you should lick your lips
before trying to eat or drink something
that might burn them.

• • •

.

Don't "go" "there."
(Or the bell will ring.)

. . .

I dreamed there was
an athletic team called
The Tokyo Infinities.
How could there be
more than one infinity?
Like, say, seventeen of them.
Maybe each member
has his own infinity.
Their uniforms were orange and black.

. . .

When Coleridge says "now" in his poem
he means now, whenever that was or is:
Now—a dim concept,
vanished in light
that vanished in the dark.

Inside

Notebook, you,
my friend,
are running out of pages.
It's time to say good-bye
to you, leaving a few blanks
at the end
for you to rest in.
For me there is no rest,
just more words
somewhere else,
my portable prison,
my life sentence
without parole,
surrounded by puns.

Notes

I'll Get It, section 12
The quotation from Tolstoy is from Constance Garnett's
translation of *War and Peace,* Modern Library edition
(New York, no date), p. 1103.

Knockouts
The epigraph can be translated either as "That seems to rhyme"
or as "That seems to make sense."
The song referred to is John Lee Hooker's "Boom Boom."

Reality
This poem is my translation of Victor Hugo's "La Réalité,"
from his *L'Art d'être grand-père* (*The Art of Being a
Grandfather*), published in 1877.

Terre Haute: For the purposes of rhyme, I have replaced
Hugo's Gonesse with Terre Haute. Gonesse is a commune
about ten miles northeast of Paris. In 1783 the world's first
hydrogen-filled balloon flew from Paris and landed in Gonesse,
where terrified local peasants destroyed it with pitchforks.
In 1923 the largest Ku Klux Klan rally ever held in Indiana
attracted a reported 75,000 people near Terre Haute.

Dombasle: Mathieu de Dombasle (1777–1843) was a French
agronomist, one of the first French farmers to grow beets to
produce sugar. Also, he invented the Dombasle plough.

Triptolemus: In Greek mythology, the goddess Demeter taught
Triptolemus the art of agriculture. He flew across the land in
a winged chariot while Demeter and her daughter Persephone
helped him complete his mission of educating the whole of
Greece in the art of agriculture.

Chlamys: The chlamys is a short rectangular cloak originally worn by men in ancient Greece.

La Vallière: Louise de la Vallière (1644–1710), who was seriously in love with Louis XIV, was his mistress for six years. The two had five children. She spent the last thirty-six years of her life as a Carmelite nun.

Silenus: In Greek mythology, Silenus is a satyr, the adoptive father of Dionysus, the god of wine and uninhibited festivity.

Paestum: Paestum was a major ancient Greek city in Greater Greece (now southern Italy). The well-preserved ruins of Paestum are famous for their ancient Greek temples, amphitheater, and city walls.

Acknowledgments

Some of the poems in this book were published in *Arc Magazine* (India), *Court Green, Limberlost Review,* and *Stride* (UK); in *Together in a Sudden Strangeness* (an anthology edited by Alice Quinn) and in Civitella Ranieri's twenty-fifth-anniversary anthology; on the *Poetry Daily* website; on the shop window of Magic City Books (Tulsa), curated by Jeff Martin; and as a broadside from Mike Heffner's Viking Dog Press. Many thanks to everyone.

Coffee House Press began as a small letterpress operation in 1972 and has grown into an internationally renowned nonprofit publisher of literary fiction, essay, poetry, and other work that doesn't fit neatly into genre categories.

Coffee House is both a publisher and an arts organization. Through our *Books in Action* program and publications, we've become interdisciplinary collaborators and incubators for new work and audience experiences. Our vision for the future is one where a publisher is a catalyst and connector.

LITERATURE
is not the same thing as
PUBLISHING

Funder Acknowledgments

Coffee House Press is an internationally renowned independent book publisher and arts nonprofit based in Minneapolis, MN; through its literary publications and *Books in Action* program, Coffee House acts as a catalyst and connector—between authors and readers, ideas and resources, creativity and community, inspiration and action.

Coffee House Press books are made possible through the generous support of grants and donations from corporations, state and federal grant programs, family foundations, and the many individuals who believe in the transformational power of literature. This activity is made possible by the voters of Minnesota through a Minnesota State Arts Board Operating Support grant, thanks to the legislative appropriation from the Arts and Cultural Heritage Fund. Coffee House also receives major operating support from the Amazon Literary Partnership, Jerome Foundation, McKnight Foundation, Target Foundation, and the National Endowment for the Arts (NEA). To find out more about how NEA grants impact individuals and communities, visit www.arts.gov.

Coffee House Press receives additional support from Bookmobile; Dorsey & Whitney LLP; Elmer L. & Eleanor J. Andersen Foundation; Fredrikson & Byron, P.A.; the Matching Grant Program Fund of the Minneapolis Foundation; Mr. Pancks' Fund in memory of Graham Kimpton; the Schwab Charitable Fund; and the U.S. Bank Foundation.

The Publisher's Circle of Coffee House Press

Publisher's Circle members make significant contributions to Coffee House Press's annual giving campaign. Understanding that a strong financial base is necessary for the press to meet the challenges and opportunities that arise each year, this group plays a crucial part in the success of Coffee House's mission.

Recent Publisher's Circle members include many anonymous donors, Patricia A. Beithon, Anitra Budd, Andrew Brantingham, Dave & Kelli Cloutier, Mary Ebert & Paul Stembler, Jocelyn Hale & Glenn Miller, the Rehael Fund-Roger Hale/Nor Hall of the Minneapolis Foundation, Randy Hartten & Ron Lotz, Dylan Hicks & Nina Hale, William Hardacker, Kenneth & Susan Kahn, Stephen & Isabel Keating, the Kenneth Koch Literary Estate, Cinda Kornblum, Jennifer Kwon Dobbs & Stefan Liess, the Lambert Family Foundation, the Lenfestey Family Foundation, Sarah Lutman & Rob Rudolph, the Carol & Aaron Mack Charitable Fund of the Minneapolis Foundation, Gillian McCain, Malcolm S. McDermid & Katie Windle, Mary & Malcolm McDermid, Daniel N. Smith III & Maureen Millea Smith, Peter Nelson & Jennifer Swenson, Enrique & Jennifer Olivarez, Alan Polsky, Robin Preble, Jeffrey Sugerman & Sarah Schultz, Nan G. Swid, Grant Wood, and Margaret Wurtele.

For more information about the Publisher's Circle and other ways to support Coffee House Press books, authors, and activities, please visit www.coffeehousepress.org/pages/donate or contact us at info@coffeehousepress.org.

RON PADGETT's *How Long* was a Pulitzer Prize finalist in poetry, and his *Collected Poems* won the LA Times Prize for the best poetry book of 2014 and the William Carlos Williams Award from the Poetry Society of America (PSA). He has also received the Shelley Memorial Award and the Frost medal from the PSA. His translations include *Zone: Selected Poems of Guillaume Apollinaire* and Blaise Cendrars's *Complete Poems*. Seven of his poems were used in Jim Jarmusch's film *Paterson*. New York City has been his home base since 1960.

Dot was designed by
Bookmobile Design & Digital Publisher Services.
Text is set in Arno Pro.